D1088856

DEMCO

animals**animals**

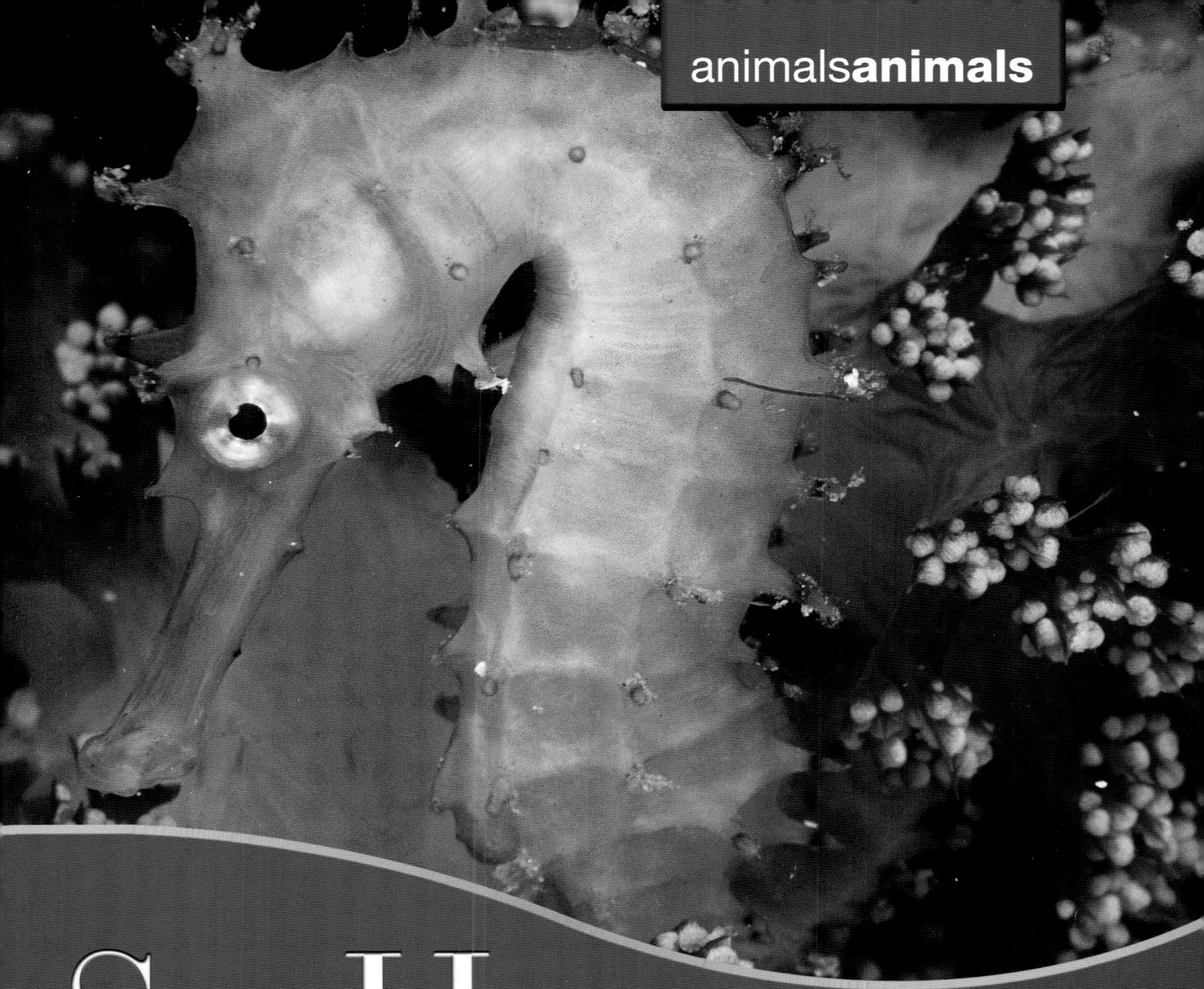

Sea Horses

by **Steven Otfinoski**

Marshall Cavendish
Benchmark
New York

Marshall Cavendish Benchmark
99 White Plains Road
Tarrytown, New York 10591-9001
www.marshallcavendish.us

Library of Congress Cataloging-in-Publication Data

Otfinoski, Steven.
Sea horses / by Steven Otfinoski.
p. cm. — (Animals animals)
Summary: "Describes the physical characteristics, habitat, behavior, diet,
life cycle, and conservation status of sea horses"—Provided by publisher.
Includes bibliographical references and index.
ISBN-13: 978-0-7614-2529-8
1. Sea horses—Juvenile literature. I. Title. II. Series.

QL638.S9O84 2007
597'.6798—dc22

2006019718

Photo research by Candlepants Inc.

Cover photo: George Grall/Getty Images

The photographs in this book are used by permission and through the courtesy of:
Minden Pictures: Birgitte Wilms, 1. Peter Arnold Inc.: Norbert Wu, 4; Secret Sea Visions, 8, 32; p. danna/phone, 34;
Brecelj & Hodalic, 40, 41. Getty Images: Stephen Frink, 11; Georgette Douwma, 16; George Grall, 17, 21, 22, 28;
Jeff Foote, 35; Jim Franco, 38; Mark Webster, 42. Super Stock: age fotostock, 10. OceanWideImages.com: Rudie Kuiter, 12,
26; Gary Bell, 33, 24. John G. Shedd Aquarium: Edward G. Lines, 13. Photo Researchers Inc.: SPL, 27.
Corbis: Stephen Frink, 36; Barnabas Bosshart, 39.

Printed in Malaysia
6 5 4 3 2

Contents

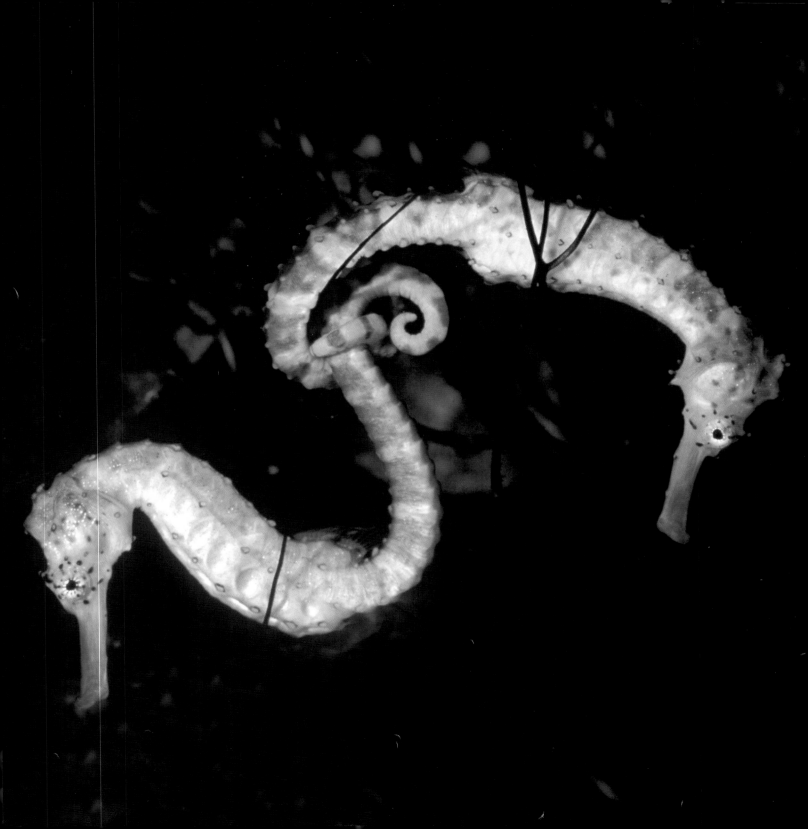

1 Steeds of the Sea

A male and female sea horse glide gracefully through a small forest of seaweed growing on the ocean floor. The two tiny sea creatures wrap their long tails around a blade of eelgrass and twirl around it like children swinging around a pole. As they spin, they show their joy by changing color. Their dull gray bodies become a bright orange in a process known as *brightening*.

The dance over, the female raises her head and snout upward. The male responds by bending his tail upward and then back down. He is pumping water out of a hole in a pouch on his belly.

This male and female sea horse are performing their fascinating courting dance.

Together the pair floats upward in the water several times. The last time, the female extends a tube, called an *ovipositor*, from her body into the hole in the male's pouch. In a matter of seconds, she places her *brood* of eggs into the pouch. Her job as a parent is finished. From this moment on, the male must tend

The female transfers her eggs to her partner's pouch using her ovipositor (left). Some weeks later, the young spring forth from the male's pouch as he pushes them out (right).

6

The sea horse's prehensile tail can grip and hold on to objects.

the eggs. He will *fertilize* them, protect them in his pouch, and in three to four weeks give birth to as many as two hundred offspring in most *species* of sea horses. The sea horse is one of the few animals where the male, not the female, becomes pregnant.

The sea horse's scientific name is *Hippocampus*, a combination of two Greek words: *ippos* meaning "horse" and *kampe* meaning "curved." The sea horse is actually a fish, even though it doesn't look like one. Its head resembles that of a tiny horse. Its large eyes can peer in different directions at the same time, like a chameleon's eyes. Its long tail, like a monkey's, is *prehensile.* It can curl around objects and hold on securely. This is important because the sea horse has no large fins like other fish. Its tiny *dorsal fin*

Using its tail, this sea horse has attached itself to a piece of coral.

and *pectoral fins* make it a poor swimmer. It is at the mercy of every passing current in the ocean. The sea horse can stay put in one spot by attaching or anchoring itself with its tail to a piece of coral, sea grass, or other object.

The sea horse does not have scales like most other fish do. Instead, its body is covered by rings of bony plates that extend to the tip of its tail. The plates act like armor and help protect the sea horse. Tough skin is stretched tight over the plates. The rigid body lends the sea horse yet another of its odd features. It is one of the few fish that moves through life in a vertical or upright position.

Sea horses evolved at least 20 million years ago. In all that time, we have learned surprisingly little about them. The ancient Greeks saw them as a mythical creature. Their sea god Poseidon drove a chariot pulled through the ocean by a giant sea horse. Later people thought that sea horses had magical properties. This may be why so many cultures have believed that the dried bodies of sea horses, when ground and eaten, are able to improve health and cure a variety of illnesses.

The sea horse belongs to a group of animals called *osteichtyes*, a Latin word meaning "bony fish." Among its relatives are pipefish, sea dragons, and pipehorses. All these fish have tube-shaped mouths, and in each case the male cares for the eggs.

Sea horses are tiny fish. The largest species of sea horse is about 14 inches (60

Did You Know . . .

About half of the thirty-three known species of sea horses live in the Indian and western Pacific oceans. Thirteen species live around Australia. Four species live in North and South America, and only three kinds inhabit the Atlantic coastal waters of Europe and the Black and Mediterranean seas.

Species Chart

◆ *Hippocampus abdominalis* is named for its extremely large abdomen or belly. It grows to 10 inches (25 centimeters) in length and lives on the southern coast of Australia and nearby New Zealand.

◆ *Hippocampus bargibanti,* also known as the pygmy sea horse (below), lives in the waters of tropical Asia and the central Pacific Ocean. It grows to 0.8 inches (2 centimeters) in length.

The pygmy sea horse.

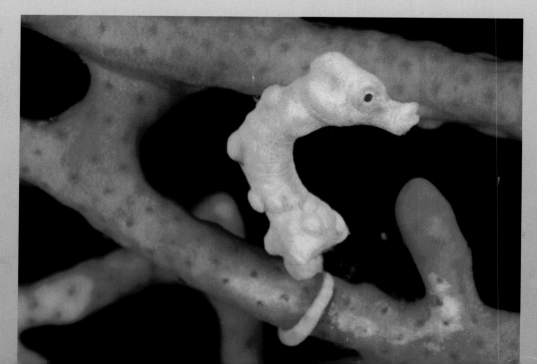

A longsnout sea horse.

◆ *Hippocampus reidi*, or the longsnout sea horse (above), lives in corals reefs in the Caribbean Sea.

◆ *Hippocampus comes* lives in the Philippines and southeastern Asia. It grows to 7 inches (18 centimeters) in length. Unlike some sea horses, it breeds year round.

◆ The tiny *Hippocampus fuscus* grows to a length of about 3.5 inches (9 centimeters). It lives along the coastal regions of India, the Arabian Peninsula, and eastern Africa.

This Australian spiny pipehorse is a relative of the sea horse.

centimeters) long. The smallest is less than 1 inch (2.5 centimeters) long. The male and female of most species are about the same size.

The sea horse lives in temperate or mild and tropical seas and oceans around the world. In the Northern Hemisphere, sea horses can also be found in rivers. In the United States, they live along the Atlantic and Pacific coasts.

Only in recent years have scientists begun to seriously study the sea horse and learn more about it. However, there are still many things about this steed of the sea that we do not know. We are not even sure how many species of sea horses there are. The number now stands at about thirty-three.

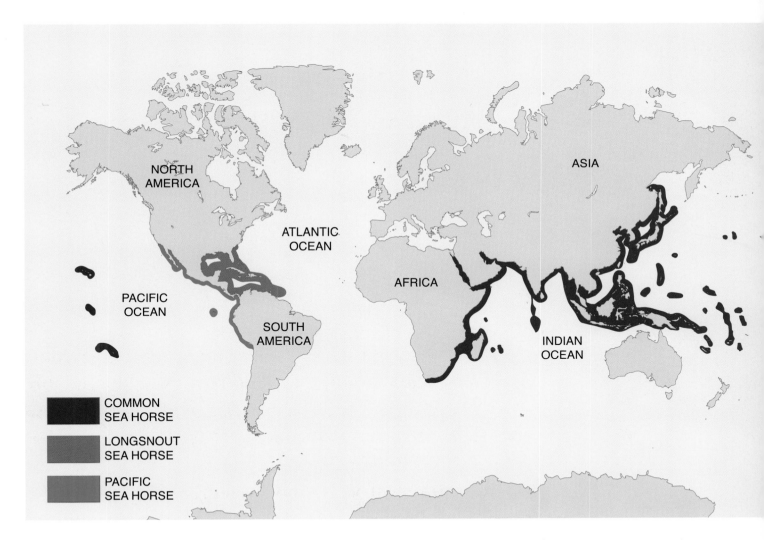

NORTH
AMERICA

ATLANTIC
OCEAN

PACIFIC
OCEAN

SOUTH
AMERICA

ASIA

AFRICA

INDIAN
OCEAN

COMMON
SEA HORSE

LONGSNOUT
SEA HORSE

PACIFIC
SEA HORSE

Most sea horses inhabit warm coastal waters. This map shows the range of three common species.

13

2 Tiny Hunters

As sunlight filters down, lending a glow to the watery world below, a lone sea horse glides along the edge of a meadow of sea grass. While many other fish swim about in large groups called schools, the sea horse prefers to swim solo. Sometimes sea horses will move about in pairs, but not often. Occasionally at night, groups of males and females can be seen gathering together. Yet the average sea horse spends much of its life alone.

When not among the sea grass, some sea horses may live among tropical trees called mangroves found along coastal areas. A third favorite habitat is coral reefs. Coral looks like an undersea plant, but is actually made up of the skeletons of tiny sea creatures.

This gathering of sea horses is fairly rare. They usually travel alone.

Sea horses spend much of their time among plants growing on the sea floor, such as this sea fan.

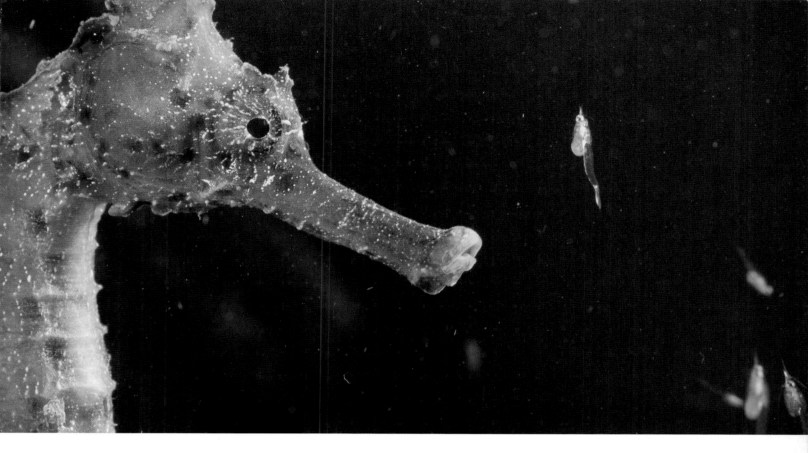

Tiny shrimp are one of the sea horse's favorite foods.

Coral reefs can be quite large and are found in shallow, warm waters.

What all three of these *habitats* share in common is a steady flow of sea life. The sea horse is drawn to these areas because they offer a regular source of food. Tiny as it is, the sea horse is a *predator.* It will curl its tail around a root, a blade of sea grass, or a piece of coral. These objects are called *holdfasts.* As it clings to the holdfast, the sea horse remains very still,

The Sea Horse:

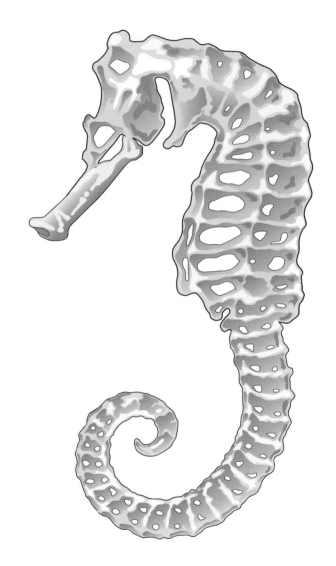

The sea horse's body is covered with bony plates that protect it like a suit of armor. . . .

Inside and Out

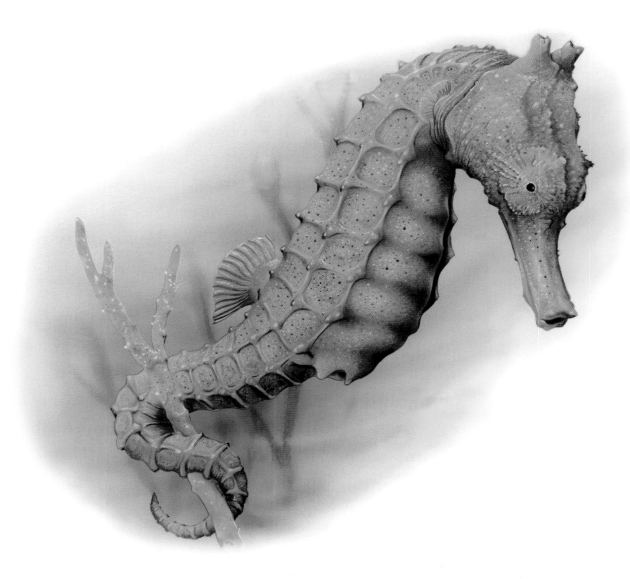

Its long snout and prehensile tail are necessary for its survival.

blending into the background of grass or coral, unseen. It then waits patiently for shrimp and other tiny sea creatures to swim by. When a possible meal approaches, the sea horse opens its lower lips and, with amazing speed, sucks its *prey* in through its long snout.

Because it has no teeth to chew with, the sea horse swallows its prey whole. The sea horse also has no stomach to digest its food. Shrimp and other prey pass directly to the creature's intestines, where they are broken down and absorbed or drawn in by the sea horse's body. What is left is then released in the form of waste.

In addition to its tail, the sea horse's other great aid in hunting is its sharp eyes. These large, bulging eyes work separately. Unlike humans and many other animals, a sea horse's eyes can look in two different directions at the same time. This allows it to search for food with one eye while watching for predators with the other.

Like other sea creatures, the sea horse generally stays within a set *home range* its entire life. In one common variety of sea

Did You Know . . .

The sea horse, although usually quiet, can make a clicking noise with part of its snout when eating. Scientists do not yet know the purpose of the noise. It may be a way of communicating with other sea horses.

The sea horse is one of the few creatures that has eyes that can look in different directions at the same time.

These baby sea horses find their father's snout a handy holdfast.

horse, called *Hippocampus whitei,* the two sexes have very different ranges. The male roams over an area of about 11 square feet (1 square meter), the size of a card table. The female's range is up to one hundred times larger. This allows the female to search for many different males during mating season. It is important that she find a mate that is strong and healthy, as it is the male who will give birth to their young.

3 Father Knows Best

Sea horses enter the world in a unique way—from a pouch on their father's belly. Their lives generally last no longer than three to five years.

The smaller species of sea horses mate when they are three months old. Larger species first mate between six months and a year, in the spring and summer. Because the male population is spread out over a large area, fighting between males for a mate is usually not necessary. But it does happen sometimes. Males compete for females in several different ways. Often two males will start a wrestling match using their tails. Sometimes they struggle to press each other against the ocean floor. At other times they use their snouts to snap at each other's gills and fins.

Sea horses are usually not aggressive, but if two males have their eye on the same mate, a fight can break out.

The male sea horse (left) is about to receive the female's eggs in his pouch. This amazing moment was captured off the coast of central New South Wales in Australia

Did You Know . . .

Out of two hundred or more sea horse offspring the male produces, only an average of two will survive to adulthood. The rest will die of starvation, be washed out into the open sea, or be devoured by predators, mostly large fish.

The winner of the contest gets to mate with the female. Unlike most fish, a pair of sea horses will remain faithful to each other for the entire mating season or even longer. One partner will choose a new mate only if the original one dies.

The elaborate courting ritual takes several days. Each morning, the female glides into her mate's home range for a visit. As they greet each other, their colors change and brighten. At their chosen meeting place, the two wrap their tails around a holdfast and swim around and around it. At one point they link tails and swim together. After about ten minutes, the female swims away. The male won't see her again until the next morning.

A newborn sea horse looks just like an adult, only in a smaller size.

Life is a fight for survival for young sea horses.

Usually on the third day, the couple is ready to mate. The female deposits her eggs into the male's pouch. The eggs are fertilized in the pouch by the male's sperm. The female returns for visits, and the two repeat their greeting dance. But for most of the pregnancy the male is alone with the eggs.

The developing offspring, called *embryos*, grow day by day. The pregnancy lasts from one to six weeks, depending on the species and the water conditions. As the time of birth nears, the male's pouch swells with the growing embryos. The father grasps a holdfast with his tail and begins to bend his body back and forth. This pumping action quickly precedes the release of the first offspring. The babies then shoot out of the father's pouch into the water. The father continues to pump, releasing a group of babies each time. The birthing process can take up to two full days. By the time it is over, the father is very tired. He will, however, mate again with his female right away. As many as three broods of offspring may be born before the mating season ends.

The newborn sea horses are about the size of your fingernail and are nearly *transparent.* Once out of the pouch, the babies are completely on their own. They will grab onto the nearest holdfast and start hunting for something to eat. They must find food soon, or they will die.

4 In Dangerous Waters

Sea horses often swim in dangerous waters. Predators are waiting, ready to gobble them up. These predators include not only larger fish such as sharks but also crabs, rays, skates, and sea turtles. Seabirds, including some penguins, eat sea horses too.

The sea horse is extremely *vulnerable* to attack. It has nothing with which to defend itself. To make matters worse, with its small, weak fins, it cannot make a quick getaway either. Its main defense is *camouflage*. A sea horse can hide from predators by latching onto a holdfast and staying perfectly still for long periods. Its naturally black or gray body often blends into its surroundings. If the background is a different

This crab, hiding in a sea anemone, is just one of the sea horse's many predators.

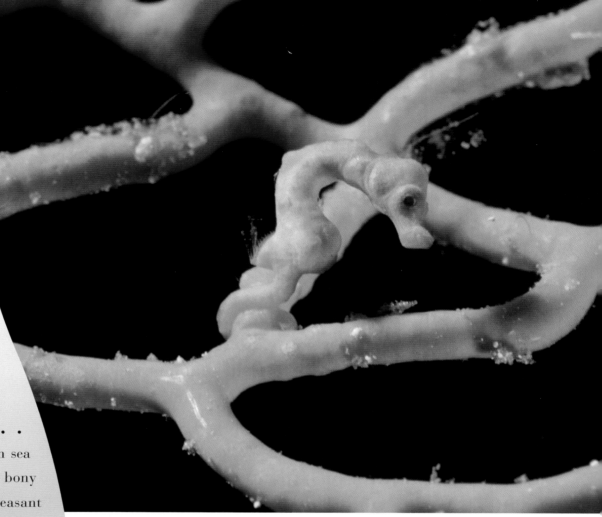

Did You Know . . .

Most fish do not prey on sea horses, because their bony bodies make for unpleasant eating.

This pygmy sea horse is well camouflaged. It is all but invisible to predators when gripping a plant stem.

color, the sea horse has the ability to change its color to match it. Some sea horses can actually produce stringy growths on their body and heads to blend in with the plant growth they hide in.

The stringy growths on the head of an Australian pot-belly sea horse make it harder to spot when it is hidden among underwater plant life.

The body of this leafy sea dragon, a relative of the sea horse, blends in with the plant life it moves among.

While predators can be avoided, bad weather often cannot. No camouflage can protect a sea horse from a violent storm. The churning waters can yank a sea horse from its holdfast and send it speeding away in the fast-moving current. The sea horse will often die of exhaustion or be washed onto the shore where it dies.

5 Sea Horses and People

Of all the predators that threaten the sea horse, none has proved more harmful than people. Around the world, fishing boats catch and kill millions of sea horses each year. Many are caught accidentally in nets meant to catch other fish and shellfish. Some sea horses, however, are caught on purpose.

Some people catch sea horses to be sold as exotic food or added to soups. Many more, up to 26 million a year, are ground up and used as an ingredient in medicines to cure various illnesses. In China, dried and ground sea horse is believed to be a miracle drug that can do everything from cure asthma to lower cholesterol. Other sea horses are killed, dried, and

People's fascination with sea horses has not stopped many of them from threatening the creature's survival.

In parts of Asia, dried
sea horse is used as
a medicine that is
believed to cure
many ills.

made into decorative objects, including pins, key rings, paperweights, and various other items.

Some captured sea horses are kept alive to be sold as pets for home aquariums in North America and Europe. Most of them quickly die in their new surroundings. Stressed by an unfamiliar environment, their immune system fails and they become prone to many diseases. Many pet sea horses starve because they will eat only live prey, such as brine shrimp.

This balm or ointment being sold in a shop in Singapore is just one of the many products made from sea horses.

Did You Know . . .
In Hong Kong, an island off the coast of China, a large species of sea horse sold for up to $550 a pound in 1997.

39

The destruction of sea horse habitats has greatly reduced their population in the wild.

Did You Know . . .

Although limits are set in some countries such as the United States, the capture and selling of sea horses still goes on in more than seventy-seven countries around the world.

They also don't usually breed in captivity, further endangering the world's overall sea horse population.

Just as harmful to sea horses is the destruction of their habitats. Mangrove stands are being drained to create land for building new homes. Warmer temperatures and disease are destroying many of the world's coral reefs. Fishing nets uproot sea grass beds as the nets are dragged along the ocean floor. For all these reasons, today the sea horse is dangerously close to becoming an *endangered* species.

What can be done to save the sea horse? It is unlikely that fishing for sea horses will be banned as many countries, especially in Asia, have a long tradition of using sea horses in medicines. Even if this

Scientists are studying the sea horse to learn more about it in order to save it from extinction.

An orange longnose sea horse floats gracefully in the Caribbean Sea.

trade in sea horses was outlawed, it would continue illegally.

The captive breeding of sea horses is another option. The science of *aquaculture* has developed technology to raise many sea creatures, including sea horses on special aquatic or water-based "farms." Sea horses bred in captivity would be healthier and better able to fight disease. They would be better suited as well to aquarium life. Sea horses raised in Asian fishing villages with aquaculture programs could be bought and sold for medicines and other uses. People would not have to capture sea horses in the wild, and populations would increase as a result.

Organizations such as Project Seahorse are working around the world to preserve and protect the coastal areas where sea horses and other creatures live. Scientists study the sea horse and how it interacts with the world around it. They then use this knowledge to educate people and to promote the health of sea horses worldwide. There is still much to be learned about the sea horse. If people around the world work together, we can save this strange and beautiful creature for the enjoyment and wonder of generations to come.

Glossary

aquaculture—The raising of sea animals or plants in a natural or controlled environment for sale.

brightening—The act of changing rapidly from a dull color to a brighter color.

brood—A group of offspring produced at one time.

camouflage—The method used by animals to conceal themselves by blending in with their surroundings.

dorsal fin—A fin on a sea horse's back that helps it move forward.

embryo—An animal in the early stage of development.

endangered—Facing extinction.

fertilize—To begin the process in which an egg turns into young.

habitat—A place where a plant or animal lives.

holdfast—An object such as a plant or a piece of coral that a sea horse can wrap its tail around to anchor itself in the ocean.

home range—The area in which an animal lives.

ovipositor—A tube extending from the female sea horse that she uses to deposit her eggs in the male's pouch.

pectoral fins—A pair of fins located behind a fish's head that aids it in turning and steering.

predator—An animal that preys on, or eats, other animals to survive.

prehensile—Flexible, muscular, and able to grab and hold onto something.

prey—An animal that is hunted and eaten by other animals.

species—An animal that shares the same characteristics and mates only with its own kind.

transparent—Allowing light to pass through.

vulnerable—Capable of being hurt or injured.

Find Out More

Books

George, Twig C. *Seahorses, Sea Dragons, and Pipefish.* Brookfield, CT: Millbrook Press, 2003.

James, Sylvia M. *Seahorses.* New York: Mondo Publishing, 2002.

Laskey, Elizabeth. *Seahorses.* Chicago: Heinemann Library, 2003.

Miller, Sara Swan. *Seahorses, Pipefishes, and Their Kin.* Danbury, CT: Franklin Watts, 2003.

Rhodes, Mary Jo. *Seahorses and Sea Dragons.* Danbury, CT: Children's Press, 2006.

Walker, Sally M. *Sea Horses.* Minneapolis: Carolrhoda Books, 1999.

Wallis, Catherine. *Seahorses.* Piermont, NH: Bunker Hill Publishing, 2005.

Web Sites

Nova Online: Kingdom of the Seahorse
http:///www.pbs.org/wgbh/nova/seahorse/

Project Seahorse
http://seahorse.fisheries.ubc.ca/index.html

Seahorses For Kids
http://projects.edtech.sandi.net/encanto/seahorses/

Seahorse Park
http://www.poost.nl/seahorse/index.html

About the Author

Steven Otfinoski is the author of books on sharks, hedgehogs, bee-
tles, spiders, and snails in World Book's award-winning Animals of
the World series. He has also written biographies of naturalists Jane
Goodall and Gerald Durrell. He lives in Connecticut with his wife, a
high school English teacher and editor.

Index

Page numbers for illustrations are in **boldface**.